CONTENTS

Introduction 1

1 Where Have I Been? 5

2 Where Am I Now? 34

3 Where Am I Going? 61

4 How Will I Get There? 104

Epilogue 149

About the Author 151

FOUR VITAL QUES TIONS

ABOUT YOUR LIFE

By Keen Babbage, Ed. D.

ISBN-13: 978-0-9982190-8-0

INTRODUCTION

This book is about you. This book is entirely about you. You are the topic of this book. You are the reason that this book exists. This book has been designed, formatted, and created for you.

The writing that has been done thus far in this book is a starting point. You will do most of the writing that eventually fills this book. Your ideas, your reflections, your memories, your thoughts, your analysis, your goals, and your plans are the essence of this book.

Four Vital Questions About Your Life extends a series of books published originally in May 2018. *Four Vital Questions for Teachers and Principals* and *Four Vital Questions for High School Seniors* offered people in each of those groups a unique book that they would become the co-author of. The four vital questions and the sub-questions in each of those books guided each reader through an individual reading, thinking, writing, and learning process.

One of the most common responses to *Four Vital Questions for High School Seniors* was that "everyone should think about those questions." Those questions are: 1) Where Have I Been? 2) Where Am I Now? 3) Where Am I Going? and (4) How Will I Get There? A thorough consideration of those four questions can be beneficial to any person, of any age, and at any stage of life.

Abundant, in-depth thinking about those four questions could be very useful in many ways such as: prior to making an important decision; as part of a process of enhancing self-knowledge; as a way to give yourself a personal retreat from the busy pace of life to a tranquil time of thought; and for an occasional review of and update of prior ideas, goals, and plans.

Another benefit of this book is that it is timeless. You can read this book now and return to the book later. Some of your thoughts about the four vital questions could be updated each time you re-read what you have written previously while other prior ideas could be confirmed.

Some of your ideas may change over time. Some memories or reflections may come to mind which were not recalled in an earlier reading. Where you are now may be different than where you were when you read this book and wrote your thoughts in this book at an earlier time. You may be ready for some new goals and new plans. You may find that other ideas are quite steady over time.

In the time between the May 2018 publication of the original two books in the "Four Vital Questions" series and writing *Four Vital Questions About Your Life* in December 2019, I experienced several events which caused me to do much thinking. At the age of 64, I started a new job which is a truly ideal opportunity and a truly inspiring experience. Changing to that job was a very smart move and may lead to additional opportunities.

Two months after starting that new job, the car I had driven for over 15 years since February 2003 needed more repairs than it had ever needed, so a decision had to be made. I sought good advice and realized that the old car needed to be replaced. Changing to a new car was another smart move, although it did take a few days to get used to the many technological changes made in cars during the 15 ¾ years since I had last purchased a car in 2003.

A few days after changing from a 2003 car to a 2019 car, I had another significant change to make. With my 65th birthday only a few months away, it was time to enroll in Medicare. The enrollment process was simple, but the realization that I am approaching the Medicare age took some time to accept.

Three months after starting a new job, three weeks after changing from a 2003 car to a 2019 car, two weeks after enrolling for Medicare, I had hernia surgery. This had been scheduled for two months so it was fully anticipated. The surgery went quite well. My family was told that it went "great." I have deep appreciation for everyone who helped with that surgery, including the people at the hospital and, especially, my dear family.

The days after the hernia surgery found me needing to move slowly and rest a lot. I would be unable to go to work until some recovery time had passed. I greatly prefer to work than to move slowly and rest a lot.

The thought came to my mind: "Keen, it is time to write the next book in the 'Four Vital Questions' series. You have had some changes in your life recently. You did a lot of thinking about your life in general and about those changes in particular. Now is the time to write the book which other people can use to consider four vital questions about their life."

I had thought a lot about this book since people began telling me that everyone should think about the four vital questions which had been designed originally for high school seniors. I had also thought a lot about the series of events which had taken me to a new job, to replacing the car I had driven for almost 16 years, to enrolling in Medicare, and to having surgery. I found myself thinking about, "Where Have I Been?" "Where Am I Now?" "Where Am I Going?" and "How Will I Get There?"

Every person who thinks about those four vital questions will have different answers based on their past experiences, their current experiences, and the direction for their future. That means this book can speak individually to each reader as they read, think, and write in response to the questions in this book. The individualized experience within this book confirms that the book is about you, is for you, and is significantly by you.

Please note that this book is written to be a personalized conversation you have with yourself. For example, when you read the question "Where Have I Been?", you are asking yourself that question. The "I" in that question is you, the reader who will read, think, and write about that question and about the other questions throughout this book.

Also, please note that this book is designed for adults from the age of mid-20s and up. That is a wide age range, but the point is that this book was developed for people with some years of, or many years of, or decades of life experiences from their adult years.

It should be mentioned that this book is not a source or a replacement for professional, credentialed, certified, or licensed guidance, advice, or counseling services.

It is my hope that reading, thinking, and writing about *Four Vital Questions About Your Life* will be rewarding for you and meaningful for you. It is also my hope that you will re-visit this book occasionally to see how your thoughts in the future may have changed since you originally worked with this book and to see which thoughts are quite firmly established. It is time for your experience of four vital questions about your life to begin. From this point forward, this book is all about you. Please let the conversation you will have with yourself begin as you turn to the next page.

Keen Babbage
Lexington, Kentucky
January 2020

1
WHERE HAVE I BEEN?

That is a big question. I have been many places. I have had many experiences. I have celebrated successes and I have endured failures. I have set many goals, some of which were reached and others have not been reached. I have revised some goals.

I have many memories from childhood and from my teenage years. I recall the transition to becoming an adult and getting out on my own. The adult years have brought a new set of challenges and of opportunities which continually get updated as life brings changes, some of which I anticipated and some of which took me by surprise.

Answering this question will work best if I divide it into a lot of separate questions which all add up to one big answer. Here goes.

First, I'll think about childhood, my teenage years and going to school. My initial thoughts are of people, including immediate family members, other relatives, friends, neighbors, teachers, coaches, and other people who impacted me as I was growing up.

When I was a child, who were the most important people in my life and what did I learn from them?

———

Person	What I Learned

Person	What I Learned

Person	What I Learned

8

When I think of all those people collectively, the most important lessons I learned from them as a group are:

———

1

2

3

4

5

6

Now, my thoughts about where I have been turn to experiences I have had. I have some strong memories of childhood and of my teenage years. There are some moments which were years ago, but which are perfectly maintained in my memory as if they happened yesterday.

The experiences which most shaped me are:

_____

Experience	Impact It Had On Me

Experience	Impact It Had On Me

Experience	Impact It Had On Me

Those people and those experiences in so many ways shaped me as a child and as a teenager. Some of the people and the experiences impacted me in ways that were not only significant then, but that last until today and may always last.

There were some challenges I had to confront and resolve when I was a child and when I was a teenager. Those deserve some thought.

Challenges	How I Confronted and Resolved Them

Challenges	How I Confronted and Resolved Them

Now, I'll think about my most valuable, most wonderful experiences from my childhood and/or my teenage years and what made those experiences so good.

Most valuable, most wonderful experiences and why they were so good:

_____

I must admit that there were some disappointments or mistakes from those childhood and teenage years. Looking back on those experiences, I can learn something that maybe back then was not so clear. The passage of time and the way things work out can sometimes result in new understandings.

Disappointment or Mistake	Lessons Learned

Disappointment or Mistake	Lessons Learned

Going beyond my childhood and my teenage years, the transition to becoming an adult brought some new experiences, some new challenges, some new achievements, a few frustrations or disappointments, and some very important opportunities. I will list some of those and what they meant to me.

Transition to Adult Experiences	What They Meant to Me

Transition to Adult Experiences	What They Meant to Me

Transition to Adult Experiences	What They Meant to Me

I made the transition to my young adult years and then built on that young adult foundation. The major events since my adulthood fully began to now, plus my thoughts about those events, are my next topic to think about.

Major Events Since Adulthood Began	Thoughts About Them

Major Events Since Adulthood Began	Thoughts About Them

Major Events Since Adulthood Began	Thoughts About Them

I need to put all of those thoughts about where have I been together in one clear summary or conclusion. It is as if I am writing the answer to an essay question about my life. Maybe I should think of what I write next as chapter one of my autobiography. Here are my overall thoughts about where have I been.

2
WHERE AM I NOW?

I am busy. I have many responsibilities. I have work to do. I have made commitments to other people and to myself and those commitments must be honored every day. I have corrected some mistakes of my earlier years. I have thought about some things I would have done differently, and I have applied those lessons. I have thought about some other things that I would not change and expect to never change. I know why those are permanent.

There are some important standards or values that I hold onto and that I expect myself to live up to. There are some priorities which I have established, and which deserve my effort daily. I am devoted to the people who are very important to me. I do a lot to take good care of myself.

I am satisfied with much of the reality of where I am now, but there is some healthy dissatisfaction which can motivate me to do better in some parts of my life. I will get to those thoughts later when I think about where I am going, but for now, it is time to concentrate on this topic – where am I now? First, I will think about my current priorities. Who matters most to me, why they matter so much to me and what I do because of that? Then, I will consider what matters most to me, why it matters so much to me and what I do because of that.

Who Matters Most to Me	Why	What I Do Because of that Priority

Who Matters Most to Me	Why	What I Do Because of that Priority

Who Matters Most to Me	Why	What I Do Because of that Priority

What Matters Most to Me	Why	What I Do Because of that Priority

What Matters Most to Me	Why	What I Do Because of that Priority

What Matters Most to Me	Why	What I Do Because of that Priority

Where am I now in terms of family relationships?

_____

Spouse

Children

Parents

Grandparents

Great-Grandparents

In-Laws

Aunts and Uncles

Nieces and Nephews

Where am I now in terms of health and fitness?

———

Exercise

Nutrition

Weight

Sleep

Avoiding harmful items or actions

Attitude, frame of mind, mental health

Where am I now in terms of work, employment, career?

———

Where am I now in terms of friendships?

———

Where am I now in terms of useful community involvement?

———

Where am I now in terms of good organizations I participate in or that I could participate in?

Where am I now in terms of promises I have made to myself and to other people?

———

Where am I now financially?

Income

Budget

Savings

Debt

Credit card use

Other financial obligations or circumstances

Where am I now in terms of what I believe in?

———

Where am I now versus where I thought I would be now?

———

Where am I now in terms of goals I previously set for myself?

———

Where am I now in terms of plans I have made for the future?

———

Where am I now in terms of my responsibilities to other people?

———

Where am I now in terms of my responsibilities to myself?

———

Overall, where am I now and how am I doing now?

———

3
WHERE AM I GOING?

Different people at various stages of adulthood will face a range of decisions, options, opportunities, and challenges. A variety of examples follow and are based on different people I know. Not all of these apply to me, but they give me some overall perspectives and frames of reference, plus they will help get me started on thinking about where I am going.

I am going to change jobs, but not soon. My current job is rewarding, and it provides sufficient income for my family and me. Still, I can tell that there are limits on my career growth at my current employer. Within two or three years, I will be at a point where to make career progress I will need to make a job change.

It might be time for our family to move. We have lived in this house for 16 years. It is a good place to live, but our family has grown from having one child when we moved here to having three. Plus, eventually my mother may need a place to live as her health has begun to decline, so she might move in with us in a few years.

He is 29 years old and I am 26 years old. We have been dating for two years. We get along so great. Our families like each other. I think he would be a wonderful husband,

and I am sure he thinks I would be a wonderful wife. We have talked about marriage. It may be time to make the big decision.

It has been 15 years since I graduated from community college. The job market has changed a lot since then. Several people have advised me to get more education. There are some certificates or licenses which could open some new job opportunities for me. It would be a major commitment of time and of money, but going back to school while I continue to work could pay off in the long run.

I need to get serious about my health. I was in really good shape back in high school. That was 30 years ago. I need to lose some weight, and I really need to exercise more. Things just get so busy that I don't give the time and effort to my health that I should. That needs to change. I must figure out what to do.

Someone asked me recently if I had thought about retirement. Well, sure, I have thought about it. I have saved some money for retirement, but I need to get more serious about that. I guess that retirement in 10 or 15 years could be managed, but I need to think a lot more about how to do that.

Years ago, I used to volunteer with a local charity that does a lot of good in this community. I have not done any volunteer work for a long time. Other things get my time now. Maybe I should start doing some volunteering again.

I have been thinking about moving to another city. I moved here about eight years ago because of a good job offer. My work is going well, and this is a good place to live, but much of my family lives back home. We keep in touch and we visit often, but as my parents get older I need to spend more time with them. If I get married and have children, I want my children to know their grandparents well. It's something I think about a lot.

I need to get rid of some bad habits. I used to read a lot, but then I just quit reading. I should start reading again. I used to eat only healthy food, but then I started eating some junk and now I eat more junk food than ever. That needs to change. I have not seen a dentist in two years. I need to get an annual check-up with my family physician. I sit around and watch too much television. I need some good habits to replace these old bad habits.

I don't hear from my friends as much as I used to. We just seem to have gone our separate ways. We all got busy. I need to reach out to those friends and get reacquainted.

There is this one local issue which really concerns me. I think the traffic system in this city is really inefficient. I attended a meeting that the city government sponsored to get citizen input on various topics, including traffic. I started wondering if I should run for the city council. I don't know much about politics, but I do know that something needs to be done about local traffic. That gives me a lot to think about.

Those examples of where other people may be going have increased my determination to know the answer to the question "where am I going?" I would like to do more than just move along from day to day. I would like to direct my path and take the steps which will get me to my desired goals. This is not something I can be selfish about because what I do will impact other people, so there are many factors to keep in mind. I've made some progress and had some achievements, but there is more that I intend to do. I have thought about that before. It is time to think about that again and to figure it out.

Where am I going with my family relationships?

———

What is good about my family relationships?

———

What would I like to see improve in my family relationships?

─────

What can I do to help make those improvements?

———

Where am I going in my work life, my job, my career?

———

What goals do I have in my career for the next five years?

———

What goals do I have in my career for the next 10 years?

———

What are my ultimate career goals?

———

How am I doing with my health?

What am I doing that is very beneficial for my health?

———

What can I do to take better care of my health?

———

Am I managing finances well?

———

What could I do to manage finances better?

———

How am I doing with saving for future expenses that can be anticipated?

———

In addition to responsibilities I have now to family and to other people, what additional responsibilities can I anticipate in the near future?

———

How well do I live up to proper standards of ethics and of integrity?

———

What is the most important change I need to make now?

———

What is the most important part of my life that needs to
stay exactly the way it is now?

———

When I think of mistakes I have made in the past, I ask
myself if I can make amends for those mistakes.
How could I make amends for those mistakes?

———

Would it do more good or more harm to re-open those old situations?

———

To what extent have I become the person I intended to be?

———

I am going to imagine myself in 10 years from now.
Who am I then?

———

Where am I going in terms of what I am doing for other people, especially for my relatives?

———

Where am I going in this community? Is there something I can do for the good of our neighborhood or of our overall community?

———

Where am I going in relation to how I live my life day-to-day? What are some small day-to-day changes I could make that would get good results and benefits? How can I be sure that making those small day-to-day changes will be advantageous and helpful?

———

If I make any significant change in my life, how can I be sure that the change will be advantageous and helpful?

———

If I do make a change in my life and it does not work, what is the best way to correct that?

———

Where am I going in terms of what I believe in strongly?
How are those beliefs shaping the way I live?

———

Have I moved away from some of my earlier beliefs? Why did I do that? Am I going toward better beliefs, or do I need to renew my earlier convictions?

———

Where I am going is based on the foundation of where I have been and where I am now. What do I need to add to that foundation before I advance toward where I am going?

———

What do I need to hold onto forever from that foundation because it is such a beneficial and essential part of who I am and of who I am becoming?

———

Overall, where am I going today? Why?

———

Where am I going during this year? Why?

Where am I going in the next 10 years? Why?

———

At the end of this day, when I reflect on the events of this day, what will I conclude?

———

At the end of this year, when I reflect on the events of this year, what will I conclude?

———

At the end of the next 10 years, when I think about the events of those 10 years, what will I conclude?

———

When I think about where I am going, what is most
important that I must make and keep as my top priority?
Why is this the top priority?

———

There is one more thought I need to add about where I am going. I need to add a list which begins with the top priority I just wrote about and which includes two other very high priorities. I cannot go everywhere. I should not try to go everywhere. Trying to go everywhere might end up with me not really going anywhere very well.

Beginning with what I just wrote as my top priority, I need to make a list which starts with that first priority and that includes two other very significant priorities, listed in order of importance.

My list of priorities which will most clearly show where I am going:

———

1.

2.

3.

4
HOW WILL I GET THERE?

I know where I have been, where I am now, and where I am going. The process of figuring out all of that has taken some time and effort, but has been very rewarding and meaningful. I know myself better than I did before I began this reading, thinking, and writing adventure. Now, having established where I am going, I need to determine how I will get there.

So far in the process of answering vital questions about my life, I have worked alone. For this next part of the process, I cannot work alone. I need to talk with people whom I trust and whom I have strong admiration for. I need to get their ideas and their perspectives. I need to know what they have learned throughout their life experiences.

For each of the three priorities that I wrote at the end of the section about where am I going, I will find two very knowledgeable people who can offer helpful ideas to me about how I implement the priority they know the most about. I may select from relatives, friends, people I have worked with, neighbors, experts in certain areas, and other people I trust. I will make sure that I talk with some people who are older than I am, so I get the benefit of what they have learned through the process of earning seniority.

For a priority on my list that relates to my career, I am going to talk with two people who have had successful careers even though they have had some occasions of frustration or failure. I need to know what they know. Perhaps their insights can help me avoid some mistakes. They may be able to make suggestions that I would never have thought of. They may know someone I need to meet.

Whether the priority is about my career or another topic, for each of the priorities on my list of the three most important priorities, I will talk with two knowledgeable people. That means I am going to have six very useful conversations. Each of these discussions will include some prepared questions and during the conversation additional questions will come up.

The prepared questions I will ask each person I talk with are these:

1. When you have made plans in your life and when you have set goals in your life for where you were going, what worked best so you got the desired results?

2. When you have made plans in your life and when you have set goals in your life for where you were going, what got in the way of your desired results?

3. Think of the most rewarding success you have earned in your life. What made that success happen?

4. Think of mistakes you have made. What lessons have you learned from those mistakes?

5. Think again about mistakes you have made. How could those mistakes have been avoided?

6. There may have been times in your life when you knew where you were going, but you had to make some changes. What made those changes

necessary? If some of those changes worked out better than what you had originally planned, how did that happen?

7. Have priorities in your life changed from year to year, or from decade to decade? What caused those changes? How can changes like those become beneficial?

8. In some parts of my life, I am not going to make any changes at all in the near future. Explain to me whether that seems reasonable to you.

9. I have three top priorities for where I am going, meaning what I would like to accomplish soon. Based on what you know, what parts of life deserve most to be given the highest priorities?

10. Before I set out on doing the work of implementing plans which will get me to where I am going, what other thoughts can you share with me?

Since this book is where I am writing my thoughts about where I have been, where I am now, where I am going, and how will I get there, a format for all the research I am going to do will help. I will start with my first priority.

Priority 1:

When you have made plans in your life and when you have set goals in your life for where you were going, what worked best so you got the desired results?

———

Ideas from first person

Ideas from second person

When you have made plans in your life and when you have set goals in your life for where you were going, what got in the way of your desired results?

———

Ideas from first person

Ideas from second person

Think of the most rewarding success you have earned in your life. What made that success happen?

———

Ideas from first person

Ideas from second person

Think of mistakes you have made. What lessons have you
learned from those mistakes?

———

Ideas from first person

Ideas from second person

Think again about mistakes you have made. How could those mistakes have been avoided?

_____

Ideas from first person

Ideas from second person

There may have been times in your life when you knew where you were going, but you had to make some changes. What made those changes necessary? If some of those changes worked out better than what you had originally planned, how did that happen?

———

Ideas from first person

Ideas from second person

Have priorities in your life changed from year to year, or from decade to decade? What caused those changes? How can changes like those become beneficial?

———

Ideas from first person

Ideas from second person

In some parts of my life, I am not going to make any changes at all in the near future. Explain to me whether that seems reasonable to you.

———

Ideas from first person

Ideas from second person

I have three top priorities for where I am going, meaning what I would most like to accomplish soon. Based on what you know, what parts of life deserve most to be given the highest priorities?

———

Ideas from first person

Ideas from second person

Before I set out on doing the work of implementing plans which will get me to where I am going, what other thoughts can you share with me?

———

Ideas from first person

Ideas from second person

Priority 2:

_____

When you have made plans in your life and when you have set goals in your life for where you were going, what worked best so you got the desired results?

———

Ideas from first person

Ideas from second person

When you have made plans in your life and when you have set goals in your life for where you were going, what got in the way of your desired results?

———

Ideas from first person

Ideas from second person

Think of the most rewarding success you have earned in your life. What made that success happen?

———

Ideas from first person

Ideas from second person

Think of mistakes you have made. What lessons have you
learned from those mistakes?

———

Ideas from first person

Ideas from second person

Think again about mistakes you have made. How could those mistakes have been avoided?

———

Ideas from first person

Ideas from second person

There may have been times in your life when you knew where you were going, but you had to make some changes. What made those changes necessary? If some of those changes worked out better than what you had originally planned, how did that happen?

———

Ideas from first person

Ideas from second person

Have priorities in your life changed from year to year, or from decade to decade? What caused those changes? How can changes like those become beneficial?

———

Ideas from first person

Ideas from second person

In some parts of my life, I am not going to make any changes at all in the near future. Explain to me whether that seems reasonable to you.

———

Ideas from first person

Ideas from second person

I have three top priorities for where I am going, meaning what I would most like to accomplish soon. Based on what you know, what parts of life deserve most to be given the highest priorities?

———

Ideas from first person

Ideas from second person

Before I set out on doing the work of implementing plans
which will get me to where I am going, what other
thoughts can you share with me?

———

Ideas from first person

Ideas from second person

Priority 3:

_____

When you have made plans in your life and when you have set goals in your life for where you were going, what worked best so you got the desired results?

———

Ideas from first person

Ideas from second person

When you have made plans in your life and when you have set goals in your life for where you were going, what got in the way of your desired results?
——————

Ideas from first person

Ideas from second person

Think of the most rewarding success you have earned in
your life. What made that success happen?
———

Ideas from first person

Ideas from second person

Think of mistakes you have made. What lessons have you learned from those mistakes?

_____

Ideas from first person

Ideas from second person

Think again about mistakes you have made. How could those mistakes have been avoided?

———

Ideas from first person

Ideas from second person

There may have been times in your life when you knew where you were going, but you had to make some changes. What made those changes necessary? If some of those changes worked out better than what you had originally planned, how did that happen?

———

Ideas from first person

Ideas from second person

Have priorities in your life changed from year to year, or from decade to decade? What caused those changes? How can changes like those become beneficial?

_____

Ideas from first person

Ideas from second person

In some parts of my life, I am not going to make any changes at all in the near future. Explain to me whether that seems reasonable to you.

———

Ideas from first person

Ideas from second person

I have three top priorities for where I am going, meaning what I would most like to accomplish soon. Based on what you know, what parts of life deserve most to be given the highest priorities?

———

Ideas from first person

Ideas from second person

Before I set out on doing the work of implementing plans which will get me to where I am going, what other thoughts can you share with me?

―――――

Ideas from first person

Ideas from second person

Having spoken with those six people, I know much more about how I will get where I am going. It took a lot of time and work to contact those people, to meet with them, to take notes as we talked, and then to think about what they said. It was worth it. I heard ideas I never would have thought of. I have much more confidence and much more certainty. I not only know where I am going, but I know how I will get there.

I need to give myself an overall summary of what I heard from the people I talked to about each of those priorities.

Summary of Discussions about Priority 1:

Summary of Discussions about Priority 2:

Summary of Discussions about Priority 3:

———

I am prepared for challenges and for obstacles. I am eager for achievements and for progress. It is very rewarding to have thought a lot about where I have been, where I am now, where I am going, and how I will get there. From time to time, I will think through all of this again. For now, it is time to put my thoughts into action.

EPILOGUE

Where have I been? Where am I now? Where am I going? How will I get there? Those four vital questions about my life have been answered. The truth is, I had thought about similar questions before, but never in such a well-organized way with a clear sequence and with a productive process. It was important to think about all four of these questions, not just one of them in isolation. The four vital questions work together, and I am glad that I got to work with them.

I will team up with these four vital questions again, probably several times, as I need to think anew about all that these questions mean and all that the answers to these questions reveal. In years to come, the four vital questions about my life and I will work together, often.

For now, it is time to take my newly acquired understanding of who I am and of who I am becoming and implement all that knowledge into useful, beneficial, meaningful action. I am prepared. I am ready. It is time for proper, wise, wholesome action that will gain the best possible results.

ABOUT THE AUTHOR

Keen Babbage, Ed. D., retired from a 27-year career in public education in 2016. He had been a middle school teacher, a middle school assistant principal, and a high school teacher. Earlier and later in his career, he worked for nine years at four private schools. He has also worked in advertising/marketing for eight years at three large companies.

He has written 22 books about education with emphasis on two areas: teaching, and school leadership/management. He has written four additional books: *Life Lessons from Cancer* (co-authored by Laura Babbage); *Life Lessons from a Dog Named Rudy; Take More Naps;* and *Life Lessons from My Grandparents.* He lives in Lexington, KY.